W9-AUY-098

9/05

A PRIMARY SOURCE HISTORY
OF THE UNITED STATES

THE EUROPEAN SETTLEMENT OF NORTH AMERICA

1492–1763

George E. Stanley

WORLD ALMANAC® LIBRARY

Please visit our web site at: www.worldalmanaclibrary.com
For a free color catalog describing World Almanac® Library's list of high-quality
books and multimedia programs, call 1-800-848-2928 (USA) or 1-800-387-3178
(Canada). World Almanac® Library's fax: (414) 332-3567.

Library of Congress Cataloging-in-Publication Data available upon request from publisher.
Fax (414) 336-0157 for the attention of the Publishing Records Department.

ISBN 0-8368-5824-7 (lib. bdg.)
ISBN 0-8368-5833-6 (softcover)

First published in 2005 by
World Almanac® Library
330 West Olive Street, Suite 100
Milwaukee, WI 53212 USA

Produced by Byron Preiss Visual Publications Inc.
Project Editor: Susan Hoe
Designer: Marisa Gentile
World Almanac® Library editor: Alan Wachtel
World Almanac® Library art direction: Tammy West

Picture acknowledgements:
The Granger Collection: Cover (upper left and lower right); Library of Congress: Cover (upper
right and lower left), pp. 4, 6, 7, 9, 10, 11, 12, 14, 17, 18, 19, 20, 21, 22, 26, 28, 29, 32, 33,
34, 36, 38, 40 (bottom), 43; National Archives: p.40 (top); U.S. Geological Survey: p. 8

Printed in the United States of America

1 2 3 4 5 6 7 8 9 09 08 07 06 05

Dr. George E. Stanley is a professor at Cameron University in Lawton, Oklahoma. He has authored
more than eighty books for young readers, many in the field of history and science. Dr. Stanley recently
completed a series of history books on famous Americans, including *Geronimo, Andrew Jackson,
Harry S. Truman,* and *Mr. Rogers.*

CONTENTS

Through the examination of authentic historical documents, including charters, diaries, journals, letters, speeches, and other written records, each title in *A Primary Source History of the United States* offers a unique perspective on the events that shaped the United States. In addition to providing important historical information, each document serves as a piece of living history that opens a window into the kinds of thinking and modes of expression that characterized the various epochs of American history.

Note: To facilitate the reading of older documents, the modern-day spelling of certain words is used.

CHAPTER 1

Exploring the New World

1492–1600

Sometime after the year 1000, Vikings from northern Europe reached what is today known as Newfoundland on the far northeast coast of North America. They didn't stay very long, and none of the other European countries knew about the Vikings' trips across the Atlantic.

Even if the other Europeans had known about the Vikings' exploration of the "New World," they probably wouldn't have been concerned. The Crusades, or holy wars, were about to begin, and many European armies were trying to recapture Jerusalem from the Muslims for Christianity. During times of truce, trade routes opened up in the Near East, which spanned across Asia and deep into Africa. In comparison, the wilderness along the coasts of North America would have held little attraction.

A lithograph, c.1840, of Christopher Columbus visiting Queen Isabella's court before embarking on his voyage. ▶

Wealthy Europeans wanted the silks, spices, and jewels that came from China, India, and the other Far East countries, but the only way to get them was to travel along a trade route across central Asia. This journey took a long time and was very expensive, and many traders returned with very little to show for their efforts.

Spain and Portugal attempted to find a less expensive way to import goods from Asia. Under Prince Henry the Navigator, the Portuguese sailed around Africa and then headed east to India. In Spain, an Italian navigator named Christopher Columbus told King Ferdinand and Queen Isabella that he could reach the riches of India faster by sailing west, and they believed him. Because they wanted Spain to become a very powerful nation, they gave him their permission to try in a document titled "Privileges and Prerogatives Granted by Their Catholic Majesties to Christopher Columbus: 1492."

PERMISSION FOR EXPLORATION GRANTED TO COLUMBUS: 1492

Ferdinand and Elisabeth [Isabella], by the Grace of God, King and Queen of Castille ...
For as much of you, Christopher Columbus, are going by our command, with some of our vessels and men, to discover and subdue some Islands and Continent in the ocean, ... therefore it is but just and reasonable, that since you expose yourself to such danger to serve us, you should be rewarded for it.... Our will is, That you, Christopher Columbus, after discovering and conquering the said Islands and Continent in the said ocean, or any of them, shall be our Admiral of the said Islands and Continent you shall so discover and conquer; and that you be our Admiral, Vice-Roy, and Governor in them ... and freely decide all causes, civil and criminal, appertaining to the said employment of Admiral, Vice-Roy, and Governor, as you shall think fit in justice, and ... that you have power to punish offenders....

We command our Chancellor, Notaries, and other Officers, to pass, seal, and deliver to you, our Letter of Privilege ... Given at Granada, on the 30th of April, in the year of our Lord, 1492.

I, THE KING, I, THE QUEEN.

THE FIRST VOYAGE

In August 1492, after receiving permission from King Ferdinand and Queen Isabella, Columbus set sail from Palos with three small ships, the *Niña*, the *Pinta*, and the *Santa Maria*. The entries in his journal of that voyage not only detail the daily problems but also show his belief in his mission.

◀ An 1893 lithograph of Columbus leaving on his first voyage from Spain.

CHRISTOPHER COLUMBUS'S JOURNAL: 1492

Friday, 3 August, 1492
Set sail from the bar of Saltes at 8 o'clock, and proceeded with a strong breeze till sunset, sixty miles or fifteen leagues south....

Monday, 6 August
The rudder of the caravel Pinta became loose, being broken or unshipped. It was believed that this happened by the contrivance of Gomez Rascon and Christopher Quintero, who were on board the caravel, because they disliked the voyage. The Admiral says he found them in an unfavorable disposition before setting out....

Thursday, 9 August
The Admiral afterwards returned to Grand Canary, and there with much labor repaired the Pinta.... Finally they sailed to Gomera. They saw a great eruption of names [sic] from the Peak of Teneriff, a lofty mountain.

Sunday, 9 September
In the night sailed one hundred and twenty miles.... The sailors steered badly, causing the vessels to fall to leeward toward the northeast, for which the Admiral reprimanded them repeatedly....

Thursday, 11 October
The crew of the Pinta saw a cane and a log; they also picked up a stick which appeared to have been carved with an iron tool, a piece of cane, a plant which grows on land, and a board.... These signs encouraged them, and they all grew cheerful.... At two o'clock in the morning the land was discovered....

Tuesday, 16 October
Set sail from Santa Maria about noon, for Fernandina.... This is a very large island.... Now, writing this, I set sail ... and search till we can find Samoet, which is the island or city where the gold is, according to the account of those who come on board the ship....

▲ An undated print depicting Christopher Columbus landing in the New World. He believed he had reached India, so he called the people he encountered "Indians."

Columbus made a second voyage in 1493. This time, because he had found some gold on the islands he explored, he was given seventeen ships and more than twelve hundred men. In a letter to the king and queen of Spain, he detailed how all the gold, which he felt sure he would find there, would be smelted and divided accordingly.

COLUMBUS'S LETTER TO THE KING AND QUEEN OF SPAIN: 1493

▲ Columbus hoped to find gold in the New World. He promised that any gold that was found would be melted down and a portion set aside for the king and queen.

Most High and Mighty Sovereigns,
… In the first place, as regards the Island of Espanola:

Inasmuch as the number of colonists who desire to go thither amounts to two thousand, owing to the land being safer and better for farming and trading, and because it will serve as a place to which they can return and from which they can carry on trade with the neighboring islands:

… That none of the colonists shall go to seek gold without a license from the governor or alcade of the town where he lives; and that he must first take oath to return … for the purpose of registering faithfully all the gold he may have found….

That all the gold thus brought in shall be smelted immediately … and that the portion which belongs to your Highnesses shall be weighed … and registered….

In reference to the transportation of gold from the island to Castile, that all of it should be taken on board the ship … [and] placed in one chest with two locks….

That the chest in which the said gold has been carried shall be opened in the presence of the magistrates of the said city of Cadiz, and of the person deputed for that purpose by your Highnesses, and his own property be given to each owner….

OTHER SPANISH EXPLORERS

Columbus made two more voyages, one in 1498 and one in 1502. Although he established Spanish colonies on the islands of Hispaniola and Cuba and explored most of the Caribbean, he would never find India or the gold and other treasures he was looking for.

King Ferdinand and Queen Isabella were disappointed, of course, but they were not disheartened. They sent other Spanish explorers, most notably Hernán Cortés and Francisco Pizarro, who began to find the riches that had eluded Columbus and to conquer and convert to Christianity the Native people in what is today known as Mexico and South America.

Still, for every Cortés and Pizarro, there were many Spanish explorers, especially Juan Ponce de León (1513), Hernando de Soto (1539–1542), Francisco Vásquez de Coronado (1540–1542), and Luis de Moscoso Alvarado (1542–1543), who explored what is now the United States and found nothing but the poor villages of the native inhabitants. A letter from Coronado to His Majesty, King Ferdinand of Spain, dated October 20, 1541, gives an account of his discovery of the Province of Tiguex, near the present-day city of Albuquerque, New Mexico.

◀ In this 1902 print, Spanish explorers Hernán Cortés and Hernando de Soto are shown with the Incas they met when they traveled to Peru to find the riches that had eluded Columbus.

▲ This drawing, c.1897, depicts the dry deserts that Coronado encountered when he explored the New World.

CORONADO'S LETTER TO KING FERDINAND: 1541

Holy Catholic Caesarian Majesty:

… After nine days' march I reached some plains, so vast that I did not find their limit anywhere that I went…. And I found such a quantity of cows [buffalo]…. And after seventeen days' march I came to a settlement of Indians … who travel around with these cows, who do not plant, and who eat the raw flesh and drink the blood of the cows they kill….

This news troubled me greatly, to find myself on these limitless plains, where I was in great need of water, and often had to drink it so poor that it was more mud than water.

The natives here gave me a piece of copper which a chief … wore hung around his neck; I sent it to the viceroy of New Spain, because I have not seen any other metal in these parts….

I have done all that I possibly could to serve Your Majesty and to discover a country where God Our Lord might be served and the royal patrimony of Your Majesty increased….

Francisco Vázquez de Coronado

OTHER EUROPEAN EXPLORATION OF THE NEW WORLD

In 1493, Pope Alexander VI had divided the New World between Spain and Portugal, but the rest of Europe paid no attention to his decree.

As early as 1497, King Henry VII of England gave permission to John Cabot and his three sons, Lewis, Sebastian, and Santius, to explore the New World and find a passage to Asia. But what Cabot found instead of the much desired trade routes were rich fishing grounds off the coast of Newfoundland.

PERMISSION FOR EXPLORATION GRANTED TO JOHN CABOT AND HIS SONS: 1497

… Be it known that we have given and granted … to our well beloved John Cabot citizen of Venice, to Lewis, Sebastian, and Santius, sons of the said John, and to the heirs of them, … full and free authority, leave, and power to sail to all parts, countries, and seas of the East, of the West, and of the North, under our banners and insignias, with fine ships … and as many mariners or men as they will have with them … to seek out, discover, and find whatsoever isles, countries, regions or provinces of the heathen and infidels … and in what part of the world … which before this time have been unknown to all Christians…. And that the aforesaid John and his sons … may subdue, occupy and possess all such towns, cities, castles and isles of them found….

Witness our self at Westminister, the fifth day of March, In the eleventh year of our reign.

An 1855 wood engraving shows John Cabot arriving in North America while searching for a new trade route to Asia.
▼

▲ An undated print of Walter Raleigh. He was chosen by Elizabeth I to establish an English colony in North America.

In 1523, Francis I of France sent an Italian navigator, Giovanni da Verrazano, to explore the eastern coastline of North America to establish claims for France. He was followed by Jacques Cartier, who discovered the St. Lawrence River, founded Montreal, and opened up French settlements. But because of political troubles at home, it would be more than fifty years before European monarchs would again attempt to colonize the New World.

After a number of ill-fated voyages by lesser navigators, Walter Raleigh obtained a charter in 1584 from Elizabeth I, Queen of England, to establish a colony in North America.

CHARTER FROM ELIZABETH I: 1584

… Know yee that … we give and grant to our trusty and well beloved servant Walter Raleigh, Esquire, and to his heirs assign for ever, free liberty and license … to discover, search, find out, and view such remote, heathen and barbarous lands, countries, and territories, not actually possessed of any Christian Prince, nor inhabited by Christian People … to have, horde, occupy and enjoy to him.… And the said Walter Raleigh … shall go or travail thither to inhabit or remain, there to build and fortify.…

Witness our selves, at Westminister, the 25. day of March, in the sixth and twentieth year of our Reign.

THE LOST COLONY OF ROANOKE

On the first voyage, Raleigh's captains found Roanoke Island, off the coast of present-day North Carolina. He named the new land Virginia in honor of the queen and then returned to England.

When Raleigh asked the queen for more money to start a colony, she agreed to give it to him, but she also asked other investors in the country to help, too. This set a precedent for colonization in North America, and in April 1585, Raleigh assembled a fleet of seven ships under the command of his cousin Richard Grenville.

When the colonists arrived in Virginia, they built a fort on Roanoke Island. But their inability to be self-sustaining and the hostility of the Indians forced the men to abandon Roanoke and return to England.

One of these men, Thomas Hariot, wrote an account that gave a view of life in the Roanoke Colony. His descriptions of the native foods were especially vivid.

A DESCRIPTION OF LIFE IN ROANOKE: 1588

... For four months of the year, February, March, April and May, there are plenty of 'Sturgeons': And also in the same months of 'Herrings', some of the ordinary bigness as ours in England, but the most part far greater, of eighteen, twenty inches, and some two feet in length and better; both these kinds of fish in those months are most plentiful, and in best season, which we found to be most delicate and pleasant meat.

— ★ —

In May 1587, Raleigh sent a third fleet to North America, which included women and children. When they arrived, they decided to remain on Roanoke. On August 18, Eleanor and Ananias Dare gave birth to the first English child born in America—a daughter named Virginia. The ships returned to England for supplies, but the country was preparing for war, so all overseas voyages were canceled.

When the ships finally returned to Roanoke, the English found it deserted—the colonists had all disappeared.

CHAPTER 2

European Colonies

1600–1640

Native Americans had been living in North America for thousands of years before the first Europeans arrived. Societies were chiefly based on kinship groups and clans, with a shaman to act as an intermediary between the people and the gods of the spirit world.

Around the time that Columbus made his first voyage, the Cayuga, Mohawk, Oneida, Onondaga, and Seneca tribes in what is today the northeastern part of the United States banded together to form the Iroquois Confederation. The laws governing the confederation were laid out in their constitution. Some European colonists saw this as a model document for their own governments. In fact, Benjamin Franklin would borrow many ideas from it during the drafting of the United States Constitution.

An undated lithograph depicts early Native Americans uniting in self-defense even though each tribe individually controlled its own affairs. ▶

I am Dekanawidah and with the Five Nations' Confederate Lords I plant the Tree of Great Peace ... in the territory of you who are Fire Keepers....

3. ... Where there is any business to be transacted and the Confederate Council is not in session, a messenger shall be dispatched either to Adodarhoh, Hononwirehtonh or Skanawatih, Fire Keepers, or to their War Chiefs with a full statement of the case desired to be considered....

7. Whenever the Confederate Lords shall assemble ... the Onondaga Lords shall open it by ... offer[ing] thanks to the earth ... to the streams of water, the pools, the springs and the lakes, to the maize and the fruits, to the medicinal herbs and trees, to the forest trees ... to the animals that serve as food and give their pelts for clothing, to the great winds and the lesser winds ... to the Sun, the mighty warrior, to the moon, to the messengers of the Creator who reveal his wishes and to the Great Creator who dwells in the heavens above....

8. The Fire Keepers shall formally ... pass upon all matters deliberated upon by the two sides and render their decision....

11. If ... the Fire Keepers ... render a decision at variance with that of the Two Sides, the Two Sides shall reconsider the matter and if their decisions are jointly the same as before they shall report to the Fire Keepers who are then compelled to confirm their joint decision....

27. All Lords of the Five Nations Confederacy must be ... men possessing ... honorable qualities....

> 66 All Lords of the Five Nations Confederacy must be ... men possessing ... honorable qualities. 99

JAMESTOWN COLONY

Because of the failure of the Roanoke settlement, England had little interest in starting another settlement in North America. But in 1606, when James I was king, he granted a charter to the London Company to colonize the New World. Captain Christopher Newport, who would set sail for Virginia, was given detailed instructions by the London Company.

INSTRUCTIONS FOR THE VIRGINIA COLONY: 1606

... When it shall please God to send you on the coast of Virginia, you shall do your best endeavor to find out a safe port in the entrance of some navigable river....

Erect a little store at the mouth of the river that may lodge some ten men ... [that] they may come with speed to give you warning.... You must in no case suffer any of the native people ... to inhabit between you and the sea coast....

In all your passages you must have great care not to offend the naturals [natives]....

And how weary soever your soldiers be, let them never trust the country people with the carriage of their weapons....

Above all things, do not advertise the killing of any of your men, that the country people may know it....

The way to ... achieve good success is to make yourselves all of one mind for the good of your country and your own, and to serve and fear God the Giver of all Goodness....

— ★ —

Although England's first permanent colony in North America was Jamestown, the London Company was really more interested in finding precious ores than in colonization. Consequently, the new settlers did not farm, and soon many began to die of starvation. Captain John Smith, the leader of Jamestown, wrote an account of the settlement's problems.

JOHN SMITH'S ACCOUNT OF JAMESTOWN: 1624

... The first land we made, we fell with Cape Henry, the very mouth of the Bay of Chesapeake....

Twenty or thirty went ashore with the captain, and ... they were assaulted with certain Indians, which charged them within pistol shot....

About the tenth of September there was about 46 of our men dead [from starvation and battles with the Indians]....

Our provision being now within twenty days spent, the Indians brought us great store both of corn and bread ready made, and also there came such abundance of fowls into the rivers....

[In January, 1608], by a mischance our fort was burned....

[June, 1608] We now remaining being in good health, all our men well contented, free from mutinies, in love one with another, and as we hope in a continual peace with the Indians....

❝About the tenth of September there was about 46 of our men dead....❞

▲ This restored settlement of Jamestown shows the type of thatched buildings that the colonists built inside the fort.

▲ A lithograph, c.1870, depicts Pocahontas saving Captain John Smith's life.

At first, the local Indians helped feed the colonists, but that stopped when the colonists began attacking the Indians and stealing their food. At one point, Captain Smith was captured by Chief Powhatan and, according to some accounts, was saved by Powhatan's daughter, Pocahontas.

After Captain Smith left in 1609, Jamestown struggled for about ten years, before John Rolfe, one of the settlers, started experimenting with a plant introduced to him by the Indians—tobacco. Soon, the colony was exporting this crop to Europe.

Even though King James I was opposed to smoking, it wasn't long before Europeans were addicted to tobacco. The planters grew rich, and Jamestown saw an era of prosperity.

PILGRIMS TRAVEL TO THE NEW WORLD ON THE MAYFLOWER

In 1620, a group calling themselves Pilgrims left England for America to escape religious persecution. They crossed the Atlantic on the *Mayflower*. Before landing in Massachusetts, they wrote a constitution, which they called the Mayflower Compact.

THE MAYFLOWER COMPACT: 1620

In ye name of God Amen. We whose names are underwritten, the loyal subjects of our dread sovereign Lord King James by ye grace of God, of great Britain, France, & Ireland king, defender of ye faith, e&.

Having undertaken, for ye glory of God, and advancement of ye christian [faith] and honor of our king & country, a voyage to plant ye first colony in ye Northern parts of Virginia do by these presents solemnly & mutually in ye presence of God, and one of another, covenant, & combine ourselves together into a civil body politick; for ye our better ordering, & preservation & furtherance of ye ends aforesaid; and by virtue hereof, to enact, constitute, and frame such just & equal laws, ordinances, Acts, constitutions, & offices, from time to time, as shall be thought most meet & convenient for ye general good of ye colony: into which we promise all due submission and obedience. In witness whereof we have here under subscribed our names at Cape Cod ye 11 of November, in ye year of ye reign of our sovereign Lord king James of England, France, & Ireland ye eighteenth and of Scotland ye fifty fourth, Anno Domini 1620.

A print, c.1932, depicts members on board signing the Mayflower Compact, as their pledge to uphold this new constitution. ▶

PILGRIMS LAND IN PLYMOUTH, MASSACHUSETTS

The Pilgrims landed on the eastern coast of Massachusetts, which was named "Plymouth" on a map made by John Smith. When they arrived, they were cold and hungry. A local Indian named Squanto fed them and taught them how to plant and grow corn and other food crops. Grateful, the Pilgrims invited their Indian neighbors to their first Thanksgiving feast. One of the Pilgrims, Edward Winslow, described the event in a letter dated December 12, 1621.

LETTER FROM EDWARD WINSLOW: 1621

Our corn did prove well.... Our harvest being gotten in, our governor sent four men on fowling, that so we might after a special manner rejoice together after we had gathered the fruit of our labors. They ... killed as much fowl as ... served the company almost a week. At which time ... we exercised our arms, many of the Indians coming amongst us, and among the rest their greatest king Massasoit, with some ninety men, whom for three days we entertained and feasted....

This 1932 print depicts the first Thanksgiving, when the Pilgrims invited the Indians to a feast that lasted three days. ▼

OTHER EUROPEAN COLONIES

Other European nations began to establish colonies in North America. The French claimed much of what is modern-day Canada. They built forts at Detroit, Pittsburgh, and St. Louis, and explored the Mississippi River valley to its mouth, where they founded New Orleans. The French were great explorers, but they weren't very interested in colonization. By 1700, only fifteen thousand French colonists lived in North America. Most of them were soldiers, missionaries, and fur trappers.

The Dutch were mainly interested in trading with the Indians, so they established a trading post on what is today Manhattan Island (New York) and called it New Amsterdam. A letter written on November 5, 1626, by Peter Schagen, an agent of the Dutch West India Company, gives a report of the arrival of one of the company's ships from New Amsterdam. Almost unnoticed at the time was his comment about how much the Dutch paid for this piece of land.

▲ A 1945 print depicting the Dutch acquiring Manhattan Island from the Indians.

LETTER FROM PETER SCHAGEN: 1626

Here arrived yesterday the ship The Arms of Amsterdam which sailed from New Netherlands out of the Mauritius [Hudson] River on September 23; they report that our people there are of good courage, and live peaceably. Their women, also, have borne children there, they have bought the island Manhattes [Manhattan] from the wild men for the value of sixty gilders, is 11,000 morgens in extent....

▲ A wood engraving, undated, portrays Roger Williams, who worked to establish peace between the colonists and neighboring Indians.

THE PURITANS

In England, a group of people known as "Puritans" decided that if they couldn't "purify" the Church of England of its Catholic traditions, they wanted to leave the country. In 1629, King Charles I granted them a charter for the Massachusetts Bay Colony. The first settlement was considered a model of piety for all. Their lives centered around their religion, and the church made all the laws.

But some of the Puritans eventually rebelled against their leadership. In 1635, a minister named Roger Williams was banished because he accused the Puritans of still being too closely tied to the Church of England. He founded the colony of Rhode Island with land that he purchased from the Narragansett Indians.

Anne Hutchinson was another colonist who challenged the strict teachings of the Puritan leadership. Well versed in the Bible, she believed that people could learn God's will without the help of ministers. This belief upset the Puritan leaders, and in 1637, they put her on trial, not only because she went against their teachings but also because women were not supposed to concern themselves with such matters. She was

TRANSCRIPT OF THE EXAMINATION OF ANNE HUTCHINSON: 1637

Mr. Winthrop, Governor: Mrs. Hutchinson, you are called here as one of those that have troubled the peace of the commonwealth and the churches here....

Mrs. Hutchinson: I shall not equivocate, there is a meeting of men and women, and there is a meeting only for women....

Deputy Governor: Now it appears by this women's meeting that Mrs. Hutchinson has so forestalled the minds of many....

Mrs. Hutchinson: I pray Sir prove it....

Governor: The court hath already declared themselves satisfied ... concerning the troublesomeness of her spirit and the danger of her course amongst us.... Mrs. Hutchinson ... is unfit for our society, and if it be the mind of the court that she shall be banished out of our liberties and imprisoned till she be sent away, let them hold up their hands.

All but three....

Mrs. Hutchinson, the sentence of the court you hear is that you are banished from out of our jurisdiction as being a woman not fit for our society, and are to be imprisoned till the court shall send you away.... We command our Chancellor, Notaries, and other Officers, to pass, seal, and deliver to you, our Letter of Privilege.... Under which same, we also command any Public Notary whatsoever, that he give to him that show it him, a certificate under his seal, that we know how our command is obeyed.

eventually exiled to Rhode Island.

As strict as Puritan society was, education was very important, and laws were passed that required everyone to learn how to read. Harvard College was founded in 1636. Its mission was to teach ministers how to explain Puritan teachings. But maintaining an ideal religious community within the settlement was impossible. The church required a rigorous examination of each individual's spiritual beliefs to determine whether he or she was worthy of being part of the Puritan congregation. This intimidating test severely limited those who could actually belong to the church.

CHAPTER 3

America Begins to Take Shape

1640–1720

As old colonies started to grow, new colonies began to emerge from them. During the 1630s, Connecticut was settled by colonists from Plymouth and Massachusetts Bay. In 1639, the New Haven Colony was established by Puritans who were less strict than the other Puritans in Massachusetts Bay. They established self-rule in Connecticut through the Fundamental Orders, which gave voting rights to all freemen and not just to church members.

New Hampshire and Maine were originally proprietorships granted not by the king but by the Council for New England. Both colonies tried to maintain their independence, but New Hampshire was controlled by Massachusetts until 1679, and Maine remained a part of Massachusetts until 1820, when it became a state.

THE FUNDAMENTAL ORDERS OF CONNECTICUT: 1639

... We the Inhabitants ... of Windsor, Hartford and Wethersfield are now ... dwelling in and upon the River of Connecticut and the lands ... adjoining ... associate and conjoin ourselves to be as one Public State or Commonwealth....

There shall be yearly two General Assemblies or Courts ... the first to be called the Court of Election, wherein shall be yearly chosen ... so many Magistrates and other public Officers as shall be found requisite....

The Governor or Moderator [of the Court] shall have power to order the Court, to give liberty of speech, and silence unseasonable and disorderly speaking, to put all things to vote, and in case the vote be equal to have the casting voice. But none of these Courts shall be adjourned or dissolved without the consent of the major part of the Court....

THE ENGLISH COLONIES BAND TOGETHER

All of the English-speaking colonies jealousy guarded their independence from each other, but Massachusetts, Plymouth, Connecticut, and New Haven eventually realized that a loose confederation of colonies might be to their benefit in fighting the various Indian tribes or in stopping Dutch expansion. On May 19, 1643, the colonies' representatives met in Boston to draft a document that outlined each colony's rights and duties.

THE ARTICLES OF CONFEDERATION OF THE UNITED COLONIES OF NEW ENGLAND: 1643

Whereas we all came into these parts of America with one and the same end and aim, namely, to advance the Kingdom of our Lord Jesus Christ and to enjoy the liberties of the Gospel in purity with peace; ... and whereas we live encompassed with people of several nations and strange languages which hereafter may prove injurious to us or our posterity. And for as much as the natives have formerly committed sundry Insolence and outrages upon several Plantations of the English and have of late combined themselves against us: ... We ... enter into a present Consociation amongst ourselves, for mutual help and strength in all our future concernments ... and henceforth be called by the name of the United Colonies of New England.

2. The said United Colonies ... do jointly and severally hereby enter into a firm and perpetual league of friendship and amity for offense and defense, mutual advice and succor....

3. It is further agreed that the Plantations which at present are or hereafter shall be settled within the limits of the Massachusetts shall be forever under the Massachusetts and shall have a peculiar jurisdiction among themselves in all cases as an entire body....

4. It is by the Confederates agreed that the charge of all just wars ... be borne by all parts of this Confederation....

66 The said United Colonies ... do jointly and severally hereby enter into a firm and perpetual league of friendship and amity.... 99

Tobacco and the Road to Slavery

In 1632, Cecilius Calvert, Lord Baltimore, received a grant from King Charles I to start a colony on Chesapeake Bay, north of Virginia. He named it Maryland after the queen, Henrietta Maria, and established the colony to serve as a haven for Catholics who suffered political and religious discrimination in England. In the end, however, very few Catholics settled there. Lord Baltimore granted large estates to his friends, which resembled medieval manors and paved the way for the plantation system.

Tobacco was the mainstay of the economies of Virginia and Maryland. Plantations were established on the riverbanks, so the wealthy plantation owners could build their own wharves from which to ship their tobacco to England.

The wealthy planters brought in large numbers of young men from England who came as indentured servants. The men traded seven years of work for their passage to the colonies. Gradually, these former servants—known as yeomanry—started their own farms. Eventually, they were replaced by slaves from Africa whom the planters owned for life, including the slaves' children.

Laws defined slavery as a lifelong and inheritable state based on race. These laws made slaves more profitable than yeomanry because planters could rely on their slaves as well as the children of their slaves.

Colonists imposed harsher punishment on their African slaves than on their indentured servants, but up until

▲ An 1834 wood engraving shows how plantation owners treated their African slaves with greater severity than their indentured servants from England.

THE ATTORNEY GENERAL'S CHARGES AGAINST SYMON OVERZEE: 1658

Mr. William Barton informs the court against Mr. Symon Overzee, for that the said Overzee correcting his negro servant the said negro died under his said correction.

... Mr Overzee commanded a negro ... formerly chained up for some misdemeanors by the command of Mr. Overzee ... to be let loose, and ordered him to go to work, but instead of going to work the said negro laid himself down and would not stir.... Where upon Mr. Overzee commanded this examinant [witness] to heat a fire shovel, and to bring him some lard, which she did and saith that the said fire shovel was hot enough to melt the lard, but not so hot as to blister anyone, and that it did not blister the negro, on whom Mr. Overzee poured it. Immediately there upon the negro rose up, and Mr. Overzee commanded him to be tied to a Ladder standing on the foreside of the dwelling house, which was accordingly done by an Indian slave, who tied him by the wrist, with a piece of dried hide, and ... that he did stand upon the ground. And still the negro remained mute or stubborn, and made no signs of conforming himself to his masters will or command.... And ... Mr. Overzee beat the negro and poured the lard on him ... till the negro was dead....

"And still the negro remained mute or stubborn, and made no signs of conforming himself to his masters will or command."

1660, there were no limits on what a master could do to his slaves. On December 2, 1658, Symon Overzee, a Maryland farmer, was put on trial for killing one of his slaves. The charges against Overzee described in detail his treatment of his slave.

This case was eventually referred to a higher court, which acquitted Overzee, after it was determined that the slave was a persistent runaway, but this case made it clear to the colonists that in order to keep the slave population under control, there needed to be new laws on how masters could treat their slaves.

THE BRITISH ESTABLISH MORE COLONIES

Under the rule of Oliver Cromwell from 1649 to 1660, English settlement was seriously curtailed in North America. But once the monarchy was restored under Charles II, colonization resumed. The king granted proprietorships in New York, New Jersey, Pennsylvania, Delaware, the Carolinas, and Georgia to those who helped him reclaim his throne.

All the colonies enjoyed a good deal of political autonomy, but they were still part of the English imperial system. In 1660, Parliament passed the Navigation Act of 1660, which

▲ A print, c.1900, of Charles II, who increased the number of English colonies.

strengthened a prior act in 1651. They espoused a policy known as mercantilism, which was a belief that

THE NAVIGATION ACT OF 1660

II. ... Be it enacted ... no goods or commodities whatsoever shall be imported into or exported out of any lands ... or territories to his Majesty belonging ... in any other ship or ships ... as do ... belong only to the people of England....

III. ... It is further enacted ... that no goods or commodities ... be imported into England, Ireland, or Wales ... in any other ship or ships ... but in such as do ... belong only to the people of England....

XVIII. ... It is further enacted ... that ... no sugars, tobacco, cotton-wool, indi-goes, ginger ... dyeing wood[s], of the growth, production, or manufacture of ... English plantations ... shall be ... transported from any ... English planta-tions to any land ... other than to ... English plantations ... [of] his Majesty....

the colonies existed only for the benefit of England.

UNREST IN THE BRITISH COLONIES

The best farmlands in Maryland and Virginia were already taken by the wealthy tobacco planters. The poor whites, the yeomanry, lived mostly on the western frontiers, and they fought constantly with the Indians, who had also been pushed inland.

About 1660, the price of tobacco

▲ An engraving, c.1760, of Nathaniel Bacon. He directed his anger toward the governor of Virginia, Sir William Berkeley, who happened to be a relative by marriage.

started to fluctuate, causing an economic depression that lasted into the early 1700s. The yeomanry were hit especially hard, and they began to get disillusioned with farming.

Virginia's government, the House of Burgesses, was made up mostly of wealthy planters, who continued to tax the yeomanry but offered no protection against Indian raids. Nathaniel Bacon, a wealthy landowner who lived near the frontier and who had witnessed both the discontent of the poor farmers and the arrogance of Virginia's rulers, joined three hundred settlers and together attacked and killed some of the Indians.

When Bacon's force grew to twelve hundred men, he decided to drive all the Indians out of Virginia. Virginia's governor, William Berkeley, demanded that Bacon stop the attacks on the Indians. In response, Bacon wrote a "Declaration in the Name of the People," in which he railed against the government and called for the surrender of Berkeley and several other Virginia officials.

Bacon and his army also burned Jamestown and even promised freedom to the servants and slaves of Berkeley's supporters. But when Bacon died suddenly, his movement fell apart.

BACON'S DECLARATION IN THE NAME OF THE PEOPLE: 1676

For having upon specious pretenses of public works raised great unjust taxes upon the Commonality for the advancement of private favorites and other sinister ends, but no visible effects in any measure adequate, For not having during this long time of his Governorship in any measure advanced this hopeful Colony either by fortifications of Towns or Trade.

For having abused and rendered contemptible the Magistrates of Justice, by advancing to places of Judicature, scandalous and Ignorant favorites....

For having protected, favored, and Emboldened the Indians against his Majesties loyal subjects, never contriving, requiring, or appointing any due or proper means of satisfaction for their many Invasions, robberies, and murders committed upon us.

For having when the Army of English, was just upon the track of those Indians, who now in all places burn, spoil, murder and when we might with ease have destroyed them: who then were in open hostility, for then having expressly countermanded, and sent back our Army, by passing his word for the peaceable demeanor of the said Indians, who immediately prosecuted their evil intentions....

Of this and the aforesaid Articles we accuse Sir William Berkeley [governor and a relative of Bacon's by marriage] as guilty of each and every one of the same....

And we do further demand that the said Sir William Berkeley with all the person in this list [nineteen other government officials were named] be forthwith delivered up or surrender themselves within four days after the notice hereof....

66 For having protected, favored, and Emboldened the Indians against his Majesties loyal subjects ...99

THE FRENCH RESIST BRITISH EXPANSION

By 1686, France controlled Ontario, most of what is today Quebec, the Great Lakes, and the entire Mississippi watershed all the way to the Gulf of Mexico. Up until that time, Great Britain had been content with the Atlantic Coast and all of Hudson Bay and the Hudson Bay watershed.

Now Great Britain felt it was time to take back the rest of the land that John Cabot had originally claimed in 1497. The Iroquois had also increased their hostilities. In a 1687 memoir, the Marquis de Seignelay laid out the dangers that threatened Canada and ways to remedy them.

MEMOIR OF MARQUIS DE SEIGNELAY: 1687

… Canada is encompassed by many powerful Colonies of English who labor incessantly to ruin it by exciting all our Indians, and drawing them away from their peltries for which said English give them a great deal more merchandise than the French…. That profit attracts towards them, also, all our Coureurs de bois and French libertines who carry their pelts to them, deserting our Colony and establishing themselves among the English who take great pains to encourage them. They employ these French deserters to advantage in bringing the Far Indians to them who formerly brought their pelts into our Colony, whereby our trade is wholly destroyed. The English … also employ the Iroquois to excite all our other Indians against us….

War is necessary….

The Iroquois must be attacked in two directions…. Three thousand French will be required for that purpose….

After having defeated and dispersed [the Iroquois], the winter must be spent in fortifying the post of Niagara, the most important in America, by means of which all the other Nations will be excluded from the [Great] lakes….

The vast extent of this country … suggest[s] the great necessity of [sending troops] throughout all parts of the Colony beyond the island of Montreal towards the great lakes which are a considerable distance from Quebec….

SALEM WITCH TRIALS

As the English colonies continued to grow, they became more and more diverse. In New England, religion re-mained at the center of people's lives. Puritan ministers like Cotton Mather not only guided their church-es on Sundays but also controlled the activities of their congregations during the rest of the week.

Anyone who violated religious communal behavior laws received swift and harsh punishment. In 1692, some residents of Salem, Massachusetts, accused their neigh-bors of witchcraft. The motivations for these allegations were economic, social, and personal. More than one hundred fifty people were arrested and put on trial. Cotton Mather gave advice to the ministers who were judges. Fourteen women and five men were eventually hanged. One man was pressed to death by stones.

In 1693, Mather published his version of the trials in *The Wonders of the Invisible World*. He describes the trial of a man known as G.B, who was accused of practicing witchcraft.

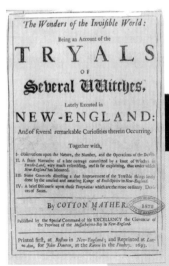

▲ Cotton Mather's *The Wonders of the Invisible World* recounted several of the witchcraft trials held in New England.

MATHER'S ACCOUNT OF G.B.'S WITCHCRAFT TRIAL: 1692

Glad should I have been, if I had never known the Name of this man; or never had this occasion to mention so much as the first Letters of his Name. But the Government requiring some Account of his Trail … to be Inserted in this Book, it becomes me with all Obedience to submit unto this Order.

I. This G.B. was indicted for Witch-crafts, and in the Prosecution of the Charge against him, he was Accused by five or six of the Bewitched, as the Author of their Miseries; he was Accused by eight of the Confessing Witches, as being an Head Actor at some of their Hellish Rendezvous', and one who had the promise of being a King in Satan's Kingdom,

▲ An 1855 painting depicting the hysteria in this trial of George Jacobs, which was not unlike the trial of G.B. as described by Cotton Mather.

now going to be Erected: he was Accused by nine persons for extraordinary Lifting, and such Feats of Strength, as could not be done without a Diabolical Assistance....

IV. ... These now Testified, that G.B. had been at Witch-meetings with them; and that he was the Person who ... Compelled them into the snares of Witchcraft: That he promised them Fine Clothes, for doing it; that he brought Puppets to them, and thorns to stick into those Puppets, for the afflicting of other People; And that he exhorted them, with the rest of the Crew, to bewitch all Salem-Village, but be sure to do it Gradually, if they would prevail in what they did....

IX. The Jury brought him in guilty: But when he came to Die, he utterly denied the Fact, whereof he had been thus convicted.

WILLIAM PENN IN PENNSYLVANIA

In contrast to New England, religious tolerance was one of the main attractions of the Pennsylvania colony. In 1681, Charles II, in repayment for a debt he owed, gave the territory between New York and Maryland to a man named William Penn. Penn in turn gave the land to his son, also named William. The younger Penn was a Quaker and believed in the equality of all men, including the Indians.

Instead of just taking the land granted to him by the king, Penn paid the Indians for it. He also preached religious freedom for all in the "Charter of Privileges Granted by William Penn, Esq. to the Inhabitants of Pennsylvania and Territories, October 28, 1701."

▲ A 1775 engraving of William Penn, who promoted equality among settlers and Indians.

CHARTER OF PRIVILEGES GRANTED BY WILLIAM PENN: 1701

… And whereas for the Encouragement of all the Freemen and Planters, that might be concerned in the said Province and Territories, and for the good Government thereof, I the said William Penn … do declare, grant and confirm, unto all the Freemen, Planters and Adventurers, and other Inhabitants of this Province and Territories, these following Liberties, Franchises and Privileges, so far as in me lie, to be held, enjoyed and kept….

That no Person or Persons … who shall confess and acknowledge One almighty God … shall be in any Case molested or prejudiced … because of his or their conscientious Persuasion or Practice, nor be compelled to frequent or maintain any religious Worship, Place or Ministry, contrary to his or their Mind, or to do or super [support] any other Act or Thing, contrary to their religious Persuasion….

For the well governing of this Province and Territories, there shall be an Assembly yearly chosen….

That the Laws of this Government shall be in this Stile, viz. By the Governor, with the Consent and Approbations of the Freemen in General Assembly Met….

That all Criminals shall have the same Privileges of Witnesses and Council as their Prosecutors….

I do hereby promise, grant and declare, That the Inhabitants … shall separately enjoy all other Liberties, Privileges and Benefits, granted jointly to them in this Charter….

William Penn actively promoted the attractions of Pennsylvania. He named the city of Philadelphia and carefully oversaw the planning and building of it. His strategy of tolerance worked. The population of Pennsylvania grew rapidly, and it wasn't long before Philadelphia was the largest city in the colonies. He governed Philadelphia wisely for two years.

Later, Penn bought more land, which eventually became the state of Delaware.

Severing Old-World Bonds

1720–1763

By the 1720s, the colonies were home to people from many countries and many religions. Each colony had its own culture, but their governments often faced similar problems.

Because the elected colonial legislatures controlled the money, including that used for governors' salaries, they were able to force the governors (appointed by the king) to support their policies. To counter this, King George II instructed the governors to request a permanent source of money to pay the governors' salaries. Most colonial legislatures reacted negatively.

SOUTHERN COLONIES

Life in the southern colonies was much different from life in the northeast. There were no big cities, except

◄ An engraving of King George II of England. He set aside land south of the Carolinas to establish a settlement for the downtrodden of England, which became Georgia.

for Charleston, South Carolina. The difference between rich and poor was greater, too, but James Oglethorpe hoped to change this. In 1732, he asked King George II for the land south of the Carolinas to create a haven for England's poor. The king liked this idea and granted him a charter, which designated this land for the poor to settle. Conveniently, these settlers would also provide a defense against the Spanish in Florida.

Oglethorpe named the new colony Georgia, after the king, and gave away the land, but no one could own more than five hundred acres, and the selling of land to other colonists

George the second, by the grace of God, of Great Britain, France and Ireland, king, defender of faith, and so forth. To all to whom these presents shall come, greeting.

Whereas we are credibly informed, that many of our poor subjects are, through misfortunes and want of employment, reduced to great necessity ... insomuch as by their labor they are not able to provide a maintenance for themselves and families; and if they had means to defray their charges of passage, and other expenses, incident to new settlements, they would be glad to settle in any of our provinces in America where by cultivating the lands, at present waste and desolate, they might not only gain a comfortable subsistence for themselves and families, but also strengthen our colonies and increase the trade, navigation and wealth of these our realms. And whereas our provinces in North America, have been frequently ravaged by Indian enemies, more especially that of South-Carolina, which ... in the late War, by the neighboring savages, was laid waste with fire and sword ... and great number of English inhabitants, miserably massacred, and our loving subjects who now inhabit them, by reason of the smallness of their numbers, will in case of a new war, be exposed to the late calamities; inasmuch as their whole southern frontier continues unsettled, and lies open to the said savages. And whereas we think it highly becoming our crown and royal dignity, to protect all our loving subjects, be they ever so distant from us; to extend our fatherly compassion even to the meanest and most unfortunate of our people, and to relieve the wants of our above mentioned poor subjects; and that it will be highly conducive for accomplishing those ends, that a regular colony of the said poor people be settled and established in the southern territories of Carolina....

and the bequeathing of farms to female heirs were strictly prohibited.

At first, slavery was also banned. Many poor people settled in Georgia, but so did wealthy planters from South Carolina, who ignored the charter and brought their slaves with them. Strong opposition to this slave restriction immediately arose, and all limitations were abolished by 1759.

The Great Awakening

By 1740, rich and poor colonists usually belonged to different churches. The wealthy planters mostly belonged to the Church of England, which did not believe that all people were equal before God. The small farmers and their families were less elitist Presbyterians and Baptists. The ministers in these churches preached that all people who believed in God were equal. To them, religion wasn't just about how to behave; it was about the conversion experiences of all men—whites, slaves, and Indians. This movement was called the "Great Awakening," and people began to realize that their religious life and their secular life could coexist separately—an idea that was completely

▲ A 1774 engraving of George Whitfield, an English minister who preached in America during the era of the Great Awakening—a movement influenced by Jonathan Edwards.

SERMON BY JONATHAN EDWARDS: 1741

... God has laid himself under no obligation, by any promise to keep any natural man out of hell one moment....

The use of this awful subject [hell] may be for awakening unconverted persons in this congregation....

And let every one that is yet out of Christ, and hanging over the pit of hell, whether they be old men and women, or middle aged, or young people, or little children, now hearken to the loud calls of God's word and providence....

... Now awake and fly from the wrath to come....

foreign to the strict Puritans.

On July 8, 1741, in Enfield, Massachusetts (later Connecticut), Jonathan Edwards preached a sermon that he called "Sinners in the Hands of an Angry God," which painted a vivid picture of someone dangling over an inferno. Edwards's feelings of faith in God caught the attention of his community.

Edwards later spent seven years at a frontier church in Stockbridge, Massachusetts, helping the Native Americans and carrying his Christian message to them as well. Other ministers helped the African slaves.

Followers of the Great Awakening wanted a way to spread their particular message to the masses, so new institutions of higher education were created. Princeton University, founded as the College of New Jersey in 1746, grew out of revivalist William Tennent's Log College. Other universities established during this religious movement include Brown University in 1764 (Baptist), Rutgers in 1766 (Dutch Reformed), and Dartmouth College in 1769 (Congregationalist).

Not all preachers of that era believed in the Great Awakening. Indeed, some of the more traditional and educated ministers denounced the movement as hysteria of the

SERMON BY CHARLES CHAUNCY: 1742

The Enthusiast is one who has a conceit of himself as a person favored with the extraordinary presence of the Deity. He mistakes the workings of his own passions for divine communications, and fancies himself immediately inspired by the Spirit of God, when all the while, he is under no other influence than that of an overheated imagination.

… Sometimes, it strangely loosens their tongues and gives them such an energy, as well as fluency and volubility in speaking.…

Sometimes, it appears in their imaginary peculiar intimacy with heaven.…

And in vain will you endeavor to convince such person of any mistakes they are fallen into.…

lower classes. Charles Chauncy, a Congregational minister of the First Church in Boston, spoke for many of them in a sermon he delivered in 1742, which tried to temper the enthusiasm of believers.

YOUNG BENJAMIN FRANKLIN

Coming from simple beginnings, Benjamin Franklin rose to become one of the most influential men of his time. In 1726, when he was just twenty years old, he left Boston for Pennsylvania and soon had his own printing industry. One of his most successful ventures was *Poor Richard's Almanack*, a collection of anecdotes and sayings of timeless wisdom. A lot of the sayings still heard today in the U.S. first appeared in this publication.

A painting, c.1900, depicting young Benjamin Franklin writing at his desk. ▶

Poor Richard's Almanack: 1747

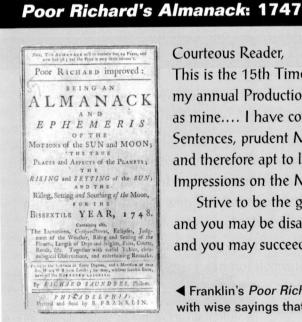

Courteous Reader,

This is the 15th Time I have entertained thee with my annual Productions; I hope to thy Profit as well as mine.... I have constantly interspersed moral Sentences, prudent Maxims, and wise Sayings ... and therefore apt to leave strong and lasting Impressions on the Memory of young Persons....

Strive to be the greatest Man in your Country, and you may be disappointed; Strive to be the best, and you may succeed....

◀ Franklin's *Poor Richard's Almanack* was filled with wise sayings that are still relevant today.

A good Example is the best sermon....

He that won't be counselled, can't be helped....

Write Injuries in Dust, Benefits in Marble....

A Slip of the Foot you may soon recover: But a Slip of the Tongue you may never get over....

Franklin believed in a good education for the youth of America, so that they could honorably and effectively serve not only the greater public but their country as well.

In 1749, Franklin proposed a method of education for young people in the colonies that differed from the religious-based schools. The proposal advocated scientific and philosophical studies that would be taught by learned men of high morals.

Franklin's proposal resulted in the creation of the American Philosophical Society in 1751, the first truly scientific society in the colonies, which would eventually become the University of Pennsylvania, the only college established in the 1700s that had no ties to a religious sect.

FRANKLIN'S PROPOSALS RELATING TO THE EDUCATION OF YOUTH: 1749

It has long been ... a Misfortune to the Youth of this Province that we have no Academy, in which they might receive the Accomplishments of a regular Education ... [and] the Sentiments and Advice of Men of Learning....

It is proposed ...

That some Persons of Leisure and public Spirit ... may be incorporated, with Power to erect an Academy for the Education of Youth....

That a House be provided for the Academy ... having a Garden, Orchard ... and a Field....

That the House be furnished with a Library ... with Maps ... Globes, some mathematical Instruments, an Apparatus for experiments in Natural Philosophy, and for Mechanics....

That the Rector be a Man of good Understanding, good Morals, diligent and patient....

CONFLICT IN THE OHIO RIVER VALLEY

For almost seventy-five years, England and France struggled for control of North America. In 1750, France's long chain of forts and settlements still dominated the interior of the continent. Most of the Indian tribes thought the British were more dangerous than the French because there were more British colonists and they took Indian land. The French usually just wanted to trade.

In 1752, fur traders from the British colonies started trapping in the area known as the Ohio Country. The French did not want these traders to gain a foothold in the region because it offered access to the French forts and settlements on the Mississippi River. To counter this incursion, the French built several fortified outposts south of Lake Erie.

In June 1754, seven of the northern and middle British colonies met in Albany, New York (known as the Albany Congress), to respond to the French move and to see how they

THE ALBANY PLAN OF UNION: 1754

It is proposed that humble application be made for for an act of Parliament of Great Britain ... [that] one general government may be formed in America, including all the said colonies ... under which ... each colony may retain its present constitution....

That the ... general government be administered by a President-General ... and a Grand Council, to be chosen by the representatives of the people....

That the President-General ... hold or direct all Indian treaties ... and make peace or declare war with Indian nations.

That they make all purchases from Indians....

That they make new settlements on such purchases....

That they make laws for regulating and governing such new settlements....

That they raise and pay soldiers and build forts for the defense of any of the Colonies....

That for these purposes they have power to make laws, and lay and levy such general duties, imposts, or taxes....

could improve Indian diplomacy. But Benjamin Franklin proposed, instead, the Albany Plan of Union, which called for all the colonies to join together as one government. The delegates accepted Franklin's plan.

THE FRENCH AND INDIAN WAR

Virginia tobacco planters received permission from the British governor to farm the Ohio River Valley. In 1754, the governor sent troops and a colonel named George Washington to survey more than three hundred thousand acres. This angered the French, who claimed this territory. They attacked and defeated Washington and his men, thus beginning the undeclared French and Indian War.

Over the next few years, the British sent more soldiers into the region, but these troops were also overpowered by the French and their Indian allies.

The French and Indian War soon

▲ Franklin encouraged adoption of the Albany Plan with this newspaper sketch.

spread beyond the Ohio River Valley. The British used their powerful navy to defeat the French, and a peace treaty was signed in February 1763.

TREATY OF PARIS: 1763

I. There shall be a ... perpetual peace ... and a sincere ... friendship shall be re established....

VII. ... It is agreed, that, for the future, the confines between the dominions of his Britannick Majesty and those of his Most Christian Majesty ... shall be fixed ... by a line drawn along the middle of the River Mississippi ... and every thing which he possesses ... on the left side of the river Mississippi, except the town of New Orleans and the island in which it is situated ... shall remain to France, provided that the navigation of the river Mississippi shall be equally free ... to the subjects of Great Britain as to those of France....

TIME LINE

1492	▪ Christopher Columbus reaches America.
1497	▪ John Cabot reaches North America and establishes English claims.
c.1500	▪ Five Native American tribes form the Iroquois Confederation.
1513	▪ Spanish explorer Juan Ponce de León comes upon Florida.
1524	▪ Giovanni da Verrazano explores the eastern coast of North America.
1539–1542	▪ Hernando de Soto explores the southeastern United States.
1540–1542	▪ Francisco de Coronado explores the southwestern United States.
1585	▪ Walter Raleigh attempts to establish a colony at Roanoke, Virginia.
1607	▪ Settlement at Jamestown, Virginia, is the first permanent English colony in America.
1620	▪ Pilgrims found Plymouth, Massachusetts, sign the Mayflower Compact.
1626	▪ The Dutch buy the island of Manhattan from the Indians.
1632	▪ The English colony of Maryland is established.
1636	▪ Roger Williams founds the English colony of Rhode Island.
1643	▪ English colonies band together under the Articles of Confederation of the United Colonies of New England.
1660	▪ The Navigation Act allows trade to benefit only England.
1676	▪ Bacon's Rebellion disrupts the Virginia government.
1692	▪ Witch trials instill fear in the people of Salem, Massachusetts.
1701	▪ William Penn promotes equality between the colonists and Indians in Pennsylvania.
1732	▪ James Oglethorpe establishes the colony of Georgia.
1732	▪ Benjamin Franklin starts to publish *Poor Richard's Almanack*.
1734–1772	▪ Era of the first Great Awakening religious movement.
1754	▪ The Albany Plan of Union is passed to forge colonial unity.
1754–1763	▪ Americans engage in the French and Indian War.

GLOSSARY

almanac[k]: an annual publication that contains an assortment of information.

amity: friendship.

attorney general: chief lawyer of a government.

autonomy: being self-governing.

Burgesses: name of the Virginia government during colonial times.

caravel: small sailing ship used by the Spanish.

charter: official grant from a government or ruler.

colony: settlement or territory owned by another nation.

commonwealth: nation or state governed by the people.

compact: agreement among people or nations.

confederacy: group of people who agree to support each other.

Crusades: holy wars undertaken at the request of a religious leader.

delegate: person authorized to represent other people.

duties: tax charged by a government on imports.

Fire Keepers: Native American gods or spirits who make sure there will always be fire.

freemen: people freed from slavery or servitude.

incursion: sudden hostile attack.

indentured servant: worker who agrees to work for a set period of time.

league: unit equal to three miles (4.8 km).

legislature: government body that makes laws.

memoir: written account of a person's experiences.

mercantilism: policy of establishing colonies for the purpose of exploiting their natural resources.

morgen: Dutch unit of land equal to just over two acres.

parliament: legislative body of a country, especially Great Britain.

patent: letter granting land to one person.

pilgrims: English Puritans who founded Plymouth Colony.

Puritans: 16th- and 17th-century group that believed in strict religious discipline.

Quaker: religious group opposed to war.

shaman: a Native American healer or priest.

Vikings: seafaring people from Scandinavia who plundered the coasts of Europe and North America from the 8th through the 10th centuries.

yeomanry: group of men who farmed small plots of land.

FURTHER INFORMATION

BOOKS

Ciment, James. *The Young People's History of the United States.* Barnes & Noble Books, 1998.

Columbus, Christopher. *The Four Voyages of Christopher Columbus.* Translated by J.M. Cohen. Penguin Classics, 1992.

Hakim, Joy. *Making Thirteen Colonies: 1600–1740*, History of US, book 2. Oxford University Prress, 1999.

WEB SITES

www.state.sd.us/deca/DDN4learning/ThemeUnits/Colonial/studies.htm
This South Dakota Web site provides links to expanded information on life and trade in the thirteen colonies.

www.apva.org/history/index.html The Association for the Preservation of Virgina Antiquities presents a detailed history of Jamestown.

USEFUL ADDRESS

The National Archives and Records Administration
700 Pennsylvania Avenue NW
Washington, D.C. 20408
Telephone: (202) 501-5404